SEEDS ON THE WIND:
JOURNEYS IN THE MINDSCAPE
By
Arianrhod Bel-Moore

GW00729960

Cover artwork by Eilis Kitts

Seeds on the Wind:
Journeys in the mindscape

Published by Lilith Mandrake Books (™Utopia Emporium)
www.LilithMandrakeBooks.co.uk
Email info@LilithMandrakeBooks.co.uk

SEEDS ON THE WIND:
JOURNEYS IN THE MINDSCAPE

'Seeds on the wind' is a small collection of initiatory patterns and pathways presented as verse – journeys in the mindscape. As you fall through the spaces in between words, lines and stanzas, may a new place of inquiry, discovery, and expansion emerge. It could be said that each piece holds keys to unlock doorways in your own mind, and trigger journeys within your own inner landscape, creating a new story, experience and pattern unique to you with each reading. It is perhaps, a form and act of mental alchemy. If you will and dare it to be!

In the Druid traditions of the British Isles, it has been long acknowledged that teller, tale and listener are forever changed by the telling of a well weighted tale, and this process has been used by those of the Bardic arts, to open gateways in the mind and evolve conscious patterns for many centuries.

The pieces in this book spontaneously arose out of the land, at sacred sites, often during or around times of ritual celebration or group gatherings, or in the silence and stillness of absolute seeming solitude. Caught from fragments whispered, sung and on occasion bellowed on the wind, reflected in still moonlit waters, glowing in moorland winter's firelight or urgently drummed up from the depths of the earth, the committing to stable form has been a response to a deep calling, an invocation and an act of sacred intent.

Each piece has its own story, some of which it is pertinent to share in order to give the canvas a context in which to hold. 'The Initiation of James' was written after an incident on the Sussex Downs at the ancient site of the Long Man of Wilmington, where several dozen people from all paths had gathered to celebrate the rites of Beltane together. During the 'running of the stag' - a sacro-magical game, a young visitor had tripped, fallen and lost consciousness for quite some time. This poem took form whilst sitting quietly on the hill, waiting for the air ambulance to arrive.

Read these poems slowly, linger in the spaces, for in them you meet a challenge and a gateway. How wide you open the door and how deep you go down the rabbit hole, is entirely your choice. Travel with open mind and light heart, fall through the spaces between, and hear the energies of time, spirit and place speak to you, unfolding a tale as unique to you as your own mind. And therein lies the magic.

So I leave these pieces humbly in your hands my dear alchemist friend, and wish you the blessings of the cool dark earth, the warm brightness of a glowing fire, the gentle flow of bright star touched waters and the freedom of air on a sun kissed, spring morning. For in each piece contained herein, you are the final, unique and magical ingredient. My sincerest blessings I place on the path before you. May you walk with grace, humour and sincerity.

Arianrhod Bel-Moore, October 2018

Poems

Plates

THE INITIATION OF JAMES

OR *"WHAT YOU SEE, DEPENDS ON WHERE YOU STAND AND HOW YOU LOOK"*

I hear a boy-man fell through a hole in consciousness and drank
from the cup of the Gods today.

I hear a man-boy danced through the realms of the Fey at the Gate of the
Ancestors, and came back safe and well.

I hear a boy-man found magic under a bel-veil inside a cauldron of knowledge
bright, in a sacred place, on a sacred site, by dancing sun and drum sung right.

I hear a man-boy fell and slipped and dove, into a sea, eternity, and met and
heard the tales of all and came back knowing, yet without recall.

I hear a man-boy went through the gates of myth into the great unknown, to
find himself found and make himself whole.

I hear he came back, and I know he is changed,
like Alice and Taliesin, new born – a mage.

And all the while a gentle song sung, from the eyes of the wren on the hill.
The holding hill, that holds all well and holds all still. She sang:-

'It's just initiation, when you fall right through
It's just initiation, The Old One's calling you.
It's just initiation, when it falls apart,
It's just initiation, straight into the heart.
It's just initiation, when unknown moves through you,
This initiation, will make you strong and true.'

The wren on the hill saw an initiation today, of a man-boy who was, for a brief
moment, touched by the Gods. She sang for him at the Gate of the Ancestors,
and was glad, for he had earned his change and was ready.
He was making himself whole.

Who knows the tales he heard, the man-boy, as he drifted in the magic heart
of all knowing, in the Hall of the Gods, at the Gate of the Ancestors? Who
knows by which tales he was touched, and to what realms he flew, as the land
drummed and the people sang and the May dance danced its round? Who
knows what this Taliesin boy-man is becoming as the returning brings grace to
his breath and gratitude to his heart.

And who would deny him this gift of the Hill? Of God's and men? Of the great
returning? 'Not I' says the wren.' I begrudge him not the fears and unknowing
that must be for and to those who stand as all stand, before the gates of
initiation. I begrudge him not his great healing and return to knowing
innocence, and I begrudge him not his song.'

So to James, the boy-man on the Hill, Wren and Raven sing and salute your return from the Gates of the Ancestors, and celebrate with us your return to the land of men, and sing your onward journey, blessed with all the hopes and promises, of the risen shining Mabon.

THERE IS A PLACE

There is a place where silence meets sound
Where sun meets the moon in the stars in the ground.
There is a place where you can lose years
Or lose your mind if your heart's full of fears.
Time loses bounds
as you fall through cracks between ground
and find yourself tumbling, illiterate and mumbling
And quite incoherent
like an innocent
A new born seeking birth
In the places in between
Where no one knows you go
Or would believe you'd been
No words may
Or can
Convey
The light of a lantern
That leads to the Fey
And what you will find
When you come to that place
Of a world between worlds
In no time and place!

'The Rhymer's Stone Rhyme!' was penned whilst visiting the stone of Thomas the Rhymer in Scotland, where it is clear both his energy and that of Lady Elphame are still easily accessible!

If you visit, please take a tiny bit of bread and a drop of Ale for him, and perhaps a little honey or a song for the Lady, and give them my regards!

The Rhymer's Stone Rhyme!
a rhyme for Thomas the rhymer

Sing me a song, yea rhyme me a rhyme, that opens the gate
That steps back in time.
Raise ye the mists, then bid ye them clear, show me the grain,
And I'll lend ye an ear.

Sing me a song, bright as the sun, yet light as the snow,
Or a light in the eye when a right truth ye know.
Sing it in silence, and rhyme it in sound, to turn it and weave it
To open the ground.
Sing me a song that sets ye apart, a song that will travel and rest in my heart.
And when I am done, remember my name, for though I'll return,
I'll not be the same.

So sing me a song and rhyme me a rhyme, that brings me back safe
Through the old gates of time.
Back through the veil from Fey Queen and Gnome, back to the tree
That's replaced by a stone.
I'll remember the words that you sang whilst I travelled,
Of tales and of secrets and of mysteries unravelled,
To bring back and share or to keep to myself,
By nod and by wink and by trust of an elf.

Rhyme me a rhyme now, sing me a song, of days and of ways
Both to come and long gone.
Show me the cycle and tread me the round,
And bind it and seal it and set it in sound.
Speak well and teach in the Circle of Spell,
That holds and enlightens and makes all things well.

Speaking the magic that falls from the trees,
That's hidden in leaf, to the power of three.
Show me the way of the five pointed star,
That shines and reveals the truth that we are.
And the lines that connect the points that are three,
Where sun meets the land, in you and in me,
They say you are dead, but here you live on,
To gift where you will a line or a song.
And honoured to meet you – such sparkle and cheer,
And next time I come I will bring ye a beer.
For sure ' tis a thing, both sides of the veil,
A smile's always raised by a good dram of ale!

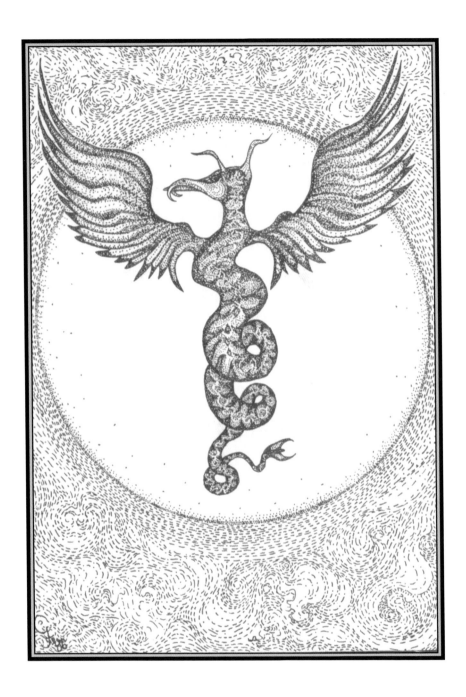

Where Dragons Dare to Dream

Have you ever lain upon a dragons back, and dove deep into where he keeps his dreams?
A golden, orange treasure trove of flashing fire-remembered burning embers, bright backed beams of light?

Have you ever breathed fire in time, with a sleeping serpentine, fire breathing sleeper
Who dreams of waking and does not know that to wake is to fall into a dream from which there is no waking for a firey, dreaming land keeper?

Have you ever climbed down the soft, sliding, slippery scaley bark of an ancient oak tree to find sleeping at its roots burning bright brimstone fire boots AND dared to try them on?
Have you ever fallen through a crack in the ground to where the rumbling sound of a dragon snoring loud bursts your ears into a thousand tiny stars so that you can hear the angels singing the fire awake in the sun?

Have you ever cared to find the keepers of the earth, of blood and of bone of sword and of stone of guarding and gaining and waxing and waning and to see what is to come?

It's not for the faint, the vain or the weak, the nervous or anxious - who daren't take a peek, but for the brave and courageous and curious and strong, on whom we depend, where our future belongs.

On Curiosity...

I wonder if everything that grows, grows because it is curious.
I wonder if everything that grows, grows because it is reaching out
to something seemingly unknown

I wonder if everything that grows, is seeking new acquaintance,
seeking connection, seeking new direction - reaching out to family yet unmet,
to say 'Hello'!

I wonder if everything that grows is seeking new heights.
I wonder if everything that grows is seeking new depths.
I wonder if everything that grows is seeking deeper, fuller, richer experience of
itself, of other and of the dance betwixt the two.

I wonder if curiosity really killed the cat,
and if so is that really the end of the story.
I wonder if lack of curiosity kills more cats.

I wonder if all roads really do lead to Rome.
I wonder if everything that grows, grows because it is curious.

I fully expect to live a rich, bountiful, expansive and wonder-filled existence
With every curious, inquisitive, seeking and searching, moving and grooving,
hoeing and glowing breath I ever take.

I wonder if the sky's the limit,
And if so, what lies beyond that?

WHERE JACKDAW SITS

This poem was written during a stay at Camelot Castle in Tintagel, where a very magical jackdaw would come to my window every morning, and accompany me on long wind blown walks. She taught me to see with her eyes, fly with her wings and journey into places far beyond. Perhaps if you decide to walk the land there, she will call to you, and give you her company you as you peel back the layers of myth, magic and mystery. A finer teacher and companion you will be hard pushed to find!

Find me where Jackdaw sits, from where she flies with beaded eye.
Blue and sharp and crystal clear, she lends me eyes from way up here.
Under Camelot's eves, arises breeze to lift her into the air,
Wind's star-crossed lover, gliding she hovers, her breath guiding and gracing
Running and chasing, as swift as the moon touched hare.
Steely her eyes, this old woman wise, she's been here before and before,
Her eyes searching mine, betwixt no place and time,
I feel she's a wily old spinster!
She calls me at dawn, like a gambling fawn, I feel in her breath youth unending
But she knows how to stand as she surveys the land, with a will sharp, strong and defending.

She shares with me her spot, Camelot atop
As we gaze out on green grey and rain
In her heart beat, I feel dancing feet
And I know we are never the same.

The Sky's the Limit
or reaching for stars

They say the sky's the limit
There is simply no truth in that
Likewise so curiosity
Most likely killed no cat.

The sky is not the limit
That is one card in a card game of lies
So throw down your Ace,
Stand up and be Grace
Oh Luminous spirit, Arise!

The sky like the mind, has no limit
It is magic that waits to unfold
So hang your heart upon a star
Don't believe all you were told!

The sky was never the limit
In it, no prison nor bars,
Reach past it and through it,
Trust it and do it
And find yourself reaching for stars!

With kind permission from British Couturier Zaeem Jamal and the 'Reach for the Stars' project
for whom this poem was commissioned.

14

TODAY...

Today I went to find a place where the dragonflies still whisper tales of Merlin on gossamer wings, where legend beats in between heartbeat, air and wing and where will unquestioning still finds it's way.

Where sleeping dragons breathed fire into my feet, making me re-join the Great Dance with increased vigour, purpose and remembering.

Where the sun watched my faltering steps with a fierce gaze, until I again found the rhythm within, swirling – even in my toenails and eyelashes, until the beat of a dragonfly's wings could be felt playing even upon my gasping, surprised breath...

Today, I went to find a place where life bursts brave and bold from the belly of death, to proudly take its place in the world – where nothing fears emptiness as it waits confident and sure, to be filled. Where the moon shines so bright, there is nothing to do but become Her, and when She is dark, there is nothing which cannot be all the more clearly seen.

Don't ask me where this place is, for grid reference or map – the secret path is known to your mind's feet.

You might well find it tucked away at the back of your mind in a dusty draw, or in a box labelled 'ancient remembering'.

Either way, you will find it somewhere safe in your own heart, placed there before your birth, whilst a thousand stars sang you into being.

Where will you go today? For what purpose? What shall you find there? I await your poem singing back to me on the wind, from a place where the Great Dance dances itself awake inside you.

STANDING STONE

Silent she stands, this sister mine
Heart of the land, beating in time
Spiralling pulses, clearing the lines
Silent she stands as I whisper in rhyme
Soft warm breath pressed to her ear
I am certain she knows me
And trust that she hears.

This Sister mine, my secrets keep
I know she will hold them and take them down deep
To where my beloved in Anwyn's deep sleep,
Shall be brightened in slumber,
Whilst sacred watch keeps.

Oh deep and deep down, on winds of time
My breath and my heart, reach to him on rhyme
And beating their way through circles of earth
I know he hears as he waits his next birth.

Though now he is held, deep in the land
I feel his heart, in the stone 'neath my hand
My feet sense his breath, and my heart, his repose
I love him and trust him, and this his heart knows.

And still she stands, my aged secrets keeping
Sharing the laughter, remembrance and weeping
For her, I sit to pen grateful rhyme, so strong and so sure
This Stone Sister, mine.

'May pole ribbons waiting for their dancers' - a contemporary expression of an ancient tradition.

The May Day Dance

This small song is included here by request. It has been used throughout the country as a calling song between men and women across the circle and during circle dances, and before the running of the stag at numerous Beltane rituals, and I am often asked for the words. They are included here so no one has to ask me again! The song alludes to the original May Day eve festivities of the 'Greenwood'.

Please use, amend and improve as you see fit, but most of all, en-joy Beltane!

We the girls, love the boys but we love them best at Beltane,
We the girls love the boys but we love them best at Beltane!

We the boys love the girls but we love them best at Beltane,
We the boys love the girls but we love them best at Beltane!
.
We the mums, fear for our sons and we fear for them most at Beltane,
We the mums fear for our sons and we fear for them most at Beltane!

We the dads, trust our lads, except of course at Beltane,
We the dads, trust our lads, except of course at Beltane!

We the girls already know the secrets of May Day Hay!
We the lads already know the secrets of May day – hey Ho!

The Owl

Night screech, come teach
Show me the pathways of silver.
Lend me your eyes, your sense and your knowing
The knowledge of cycles of reaping and sowing
Show me the trackways of which many are wary
Seen oft most by those with a kinship with faery
Gliding and sensing the trackways of old
The lines on which stories were sung, stored and told

Show me the lines which sing to me still
And teach me to know, to dare and to will
And walking the path by the silvery moon
To hold dear my silence, and honour the quill

'The Hag's Chair' is one of several pieces which were dictated with urgency, speed and a great deal of power, on location at Loughcrew in Ireland, at the seat of the Cailleach's throne – or the Hag's Chair.

The spirits of the land, of people and of place are very strong here, and it has been the site of many magical occurrences for the groups I have had the privilege to work with on site. Her voice speaks through the strangest of mediums there, and with very direct force.

Please do read this slowly, and if at all possible, you might like to read the story of the Cailleach from this region, and spend a little time connecting with this image of the site itself before reading the poem, then let the words transport you to and through the veil there, which is so very easily rendered.

The Hag's Chair

Which witch is which, who on Her throne sits, on a hill to the East at
Loughcrew?
Which witch is which, who grants you a wish,
If you sit where her magic runs true?
Which witch is which, is she Maeve or Wauru, and what would you do,
if your wish then came true?
And whoever she be – maybe Queen of the Sidhe, what means she to you,
and what means she to me?
Whether witch or fair Queen, what does her throne mean, in this time on this
day, midst the green and the grey,
By Moon and by Sun is old magic begun,
and by night and day doth increase, spin and abay.

What means it to sit, where Witch, Modron, Queen their dictates have made
And their wild wisdom seen?
Where laws of the earth, of life death and birth,
churn rise and spin to the magic within
Then turn round about and spiralling out show what's yet to come,
is now, and has been.

In this day, at this hour, can you feel their power, the Ancestors call deep in you?
If you feel magic rise, then sit, close your eyes, and climb the blessed road,
which is steep
Where hawk's secrets keep, to eager your feet in the place
where her magic runs deep.
Next eye of the storm on an equinox morn,
feel your soul rise and wake from it's sleep.
By the eye of the moon, let her sing you her tune,
let her stones call you on through the ages
Call out her name, and return her refrain, to open the doors of the sages.

So find your way there, to Our Lady's chair,
and find what's to be found deep in you.
Magic there find if you'll open your mind, and for those with the heart,
the door to the Art
Mid the bones and the stones of Loughcrew.

Which witch is which, by blood and by bone, you may ask of yourself
as you sit on Her throne
And which witch is which, you may ask in your head,
is she living or dead – or coming alive deep within you?
This you may ask, as you tend to your task, on a Hill to the East of Loughcrew.

24

CIRCLE OF STONE

Circle of stone, my hilltop home
The poet and bard declared.
By wind from the West, at Spirit's behest
A soul's strengthened and nurtured and bared.

Dancing a round between silence and sound,
soft grass on the hill speaks in rhyme still
By mighty winds gale so unfolds the tale, as the birds and the oceans keep time.
As mist rolls in by sylph and by djinn, the magic it steadily rouses
Sends birds to the ground, as wild winds abound,
sending folks in their droves to their houses.

Wild sings the wind to poet on hill, to interpret and listen and fashion at will
Fast comes the next strand, to weave song from the land,
words soft like a bird in her hand.

Deep trenches of stone of rock and of bone, constant and true and unending
Rains on coast, hill and plain through cycles remain
yet the circle stands strong safe and still.

In labyrinth of grass, bard fashions her task, her face feels no sting of the rain.
Soft hidden in grass, she completes her task,
her thoughts- spiralling motion – a train!
Straight from Earth's heart, she weaves sacred art,
and will leave never being the same.

For in words lay the power, to make brave hearts cower,
or strengthen the hearts of the weak.
For in wisdom's soft train, like startling rain, the healing and magic's unique.
And words well thought upon, help a soul move along,
and connect to the song of the land.
There's no right or wrong, in one heart belong,
from beginning to end is this song.

DAUGHTER OF MERLIN

I call to the Ancient Ones
I call to the wise
I call through turbulent, thundering skies
I call to my kith and I call to my kin
I call from without, I call deep within

For Daughter of Merlin am I
Child of this land and this sky
Weaving a circle in sound
Dancing feet spiral the ground
The fate of these Isles at stake
Into the dream I awake

Calling to Power of Land
Held within Mighty One's hand
Raise fast the power in my veins
Power of torrential rains
Call up the Power of Stone
The Power to face all alone

For Daughter of Merlin am I
Child of sea and of sky
Standing on Ancestor's Shield
The Power of Place now I wield

For Daughter of Merlin am I
And so shall I be till I die.

The three-fold dance!

I call to the ancient ones, the crones that I have been
I call to the maiden and the mother, within
I call to the bright- eyed maid
I call the one-eyed hag
I call to the mysteries
I call my magic back

This trescele I have danced before
Its mysteries I have seen
For Mother Maiden Crone I am –
And always have been.

FAIRIES

(For Ralph Harvey and his book *'The Good People'* – Capall Bann)

You once asked if I believe in fairies.
I think I gave you a smile.
I decided not to answer,
But to walk in the glade a while.

You asked what I thought about fairies,
I continued as if I'd not heard,
I thought I'd let someone else speak -
So I let crow, that 'crafty' old bird!

You asked if I believe in fairies,
and whether I'd care to reply,
I sat on a stone by a babbling brook,
And I told you I would, by and by.

You asked if I believe in fairies,
And you let out a well-worn sigh,
To say 'yes' at your behest, might spoil your quest
To say 'no' would my friend, be a lie!

The truth is my dear, your eyes dimmed with fear
Are blind to the truth of that realm.
You ask of 'The Art' but it's all about 'Heart'
If only you saw they were there.

So, I breathing the laughter of the little one's round
As they danced by your feet on the ground,
When they winked, then I knew, took their lead and their cue,
When I spoke by and by, this was my reply

'Do you think fairies, believe in you'

Moon Hare

Moon touched hare
Bare
Dare
Dare to bare, box - gloves off
Socks, tunnel, rabbit hole
Time, watch, Alice, stole
Stop, smell, listen, leap
Stare and stop, then dart then leap

Silver slivered bright eyed burst
Witch's friend and witch's curse
Fur-lined flurry of fastness
Outlined silver in darkness
Darting now quickly you passed us
Your legend will ever outlast us
Flash of ethereal, moonlight glow
We follow deeper down the rabbit hole
Still as rock then fast as air
The legend of the mysterious, moon kissed hare.

YAN A DICK, TAN A DICK!

This is a short song which is well known in certain quarters and sung to a particular stone in the complex of Avebury. The song uses an old sheep counting system (I have heard many hilarious attributes for the words of this rhyme, but can assure you, seeing as I wrote it, the verse is not an old English magical formula - it is in fact based on a system for counting sheep!)

The purpose of the rhyme is to align with the stone's power and use it as an affirmation and grounding for the intention to speak and hold to your truth, or remain silent. The first part of the song locates the stone - so if you can work out which is Harry's stone and which way round we are working, and where we are starting, you should have no problem locating the correct stone!

> Yan a dick Tan a dick toil an' tarry
> Third stone along from the stone from Harry
> Yan a dick tan a dick come what may
> My yes is my yes and my nay is my nay!

The interesting thing with this little piece is that if you can hit a rhyme that works for you, you will find it builds a power, and really can help you stand strong, mean what you say or otherwise keep your own counsel!

THE KNOTTING SONG INTRO

This is a little piece of Celtic magic! Knot magic uses focused intent to bind energy patterns into a substance, for a myriad of purposes. This song is for the knotting of a cord girdle of empowerment, to assist work with your own life force, fate path and purpose, by affirming and surrounding yourself with a set of characteristics and qualities to help you meet any challenge life puts across your path.

The method is simple. Clear your mind and space, focus your will. Take either a single piece of chord, or 3 equal length strands (representing past, present and future), and tie a first knot, pulling in the power of the first knot (courage) from land beneath you, the sky above you and your ancestral lines on both sides, and weave all that power into the first knot. Then continue with each knot. On every 'celebration of self/claiming of honour' you might like to weave a special bead or token into your girdle to represent the sacredness of your existence, your commitment to your own path and your acceptance of yourself, and your place within your own line of ancestors.

This part of the ritual is important as a re-claiming of your sacredness and honour back through your ancestral and spiritual lineages. *The Wiccan Rede*, if you have not come across it before, is a beautiful code of conduct – a modern construct rooted in ancient values. It is worth looking up if you are not familiar with it.

Enjoy the process, make it your own. (I have a song I have set the knotting to, which helps focus intention and power for me – experiment and see what works for you.)

Finally, either tie the girdle around your waist, hang it somewhere you can see it or keep it to put under your pillow when you feel the need. May it affirm the light within you, the core powers which flow through it, and may the powers of courage, youth, wisdom, truth, temperance, bliss, light and love surround you, uphold you and flow through you.

You are welcome to send your experiences with this little ritual, to the publisher – I would love to hear how you get on! And yes, a small spell book is on its way, due for release May 2019.

THE KNOTTING SONG

The first knot is courage
The second knot is youth
The third knot is wisdom deep
The fourth knot is truth

And I celebrate my life, and I claim my honour now
These words the Wiccan Rede fulfil
An' it harm none, do what you will!

The fifth knot is temperance
The sixth knot is bliss
The seventh knot your light from within
The eighth knot, a kiss

And I celebrate my life, and I claim my honour now
These words the Wiccan Rede fulfil
An' it harm none, do what ye will, and it harm none, do what ye will

This image shows a Celtic knot spell in the same tradition, in this instance, a healing knot spell hanging from the Holy Thorn in Glastonbury.

From high on the hill overlooking Merlin's Cave in Tintagel, where legends of Arthur and Merlin sing through seemingly silent stone, orchestrated by memories long held in the sacred waters of cove, and witnessed in hushed, stolen whispers on the wind.

THE LAND SPEAKS...

The land speaks, the land of my heart,
The land of my fathers, the land of my art.
The land speaks, windswept and wild
Unruly and raw and keeps me beguiled.
Enchanted and mystical shapes unfold
Revealing their stories as histories are told.

The magic of fey calls from Merlin's damp cove,
Whilst magical feet dance in soft heather grove.
From out of the sea, each island arising
Soft voices call, the caller disguising
Shadows and shapes move on stony black wall
Legends of kings and of rise and of fall.

Knights on horses, fast water courses
Galloping memories to sea
Defenders defend, as rocks never end
And infidels head North and flee.
By moon and by sun, old tales spun

Beginnings new and endings undone
In this sacred place, by nine times nine, the land speaks soft
both its tale and mine
In the silence of heather and storm cloud and weather,
All ends here before its begun!

CHANGE...

We will sit by the sea, you and I
Watching the colours that well
And I recall sitting here yesterday, and the stories that then you did tell...
You spoke of the sea, as green as the earth,
You spoke of the sea that was flat
You spoke of a sea, like a mill pond clear,
I remember for sure you said that!

And as we sit here, in the mist and the grey,
The water's most certainly brown.
And the surface is blown and exploded within,
By the furious North wind's frown.

But yesterday you told me,
And of this I am quite sure,
That the water was still, quiet, serene and totally green
With hints that were white, grey and pure.
For you see it is true, the sea my friend
Is like unto life, love and men

One day green, one day grey, then brown to green again

About the Author

Arianrhod Bel-Moore is a commercial writer who lives and works in the quiet places, or as she calls them, the 'places between'. Her work is inspired by the natural rhythms and cycles of the seasons, of the celestial bodies and the mysteries, myths, magic and legends of the land and its people. She lives in quiet seclusion, finding her inspiration in the mountains of Snowdonia, upon the' Shining trackways' across the UK, and the rugged wild of Inys Mon.

Seeds on the Wind – Acknowledgements

There are several people without whom this book would not have been possible in its present form. I owe them each a debt of gratitude far greater than can be conveyed here, and that gratitude makes it's way through the ether to them with every breath.

They are:

Lilith Mandrake for all the hand holding, butt kicking, humour, patience, discretion and expertise, long time friend and adventurer Ralph Harvey, the inspirational photographer and legend that is Billie Scheepers, the sublimely talented artistes Courtney Davis, Eilis Kitts, Jolyon Ward, Rowan Wulfe and Richard Gordon for their exceptional contributions not just to this book, but to inspirational art and humanity in general – the world is a brighter, more balanced and kinder place because of you.

A very quiet 'thank you' to the 'Eminent Zeminent', who knows exactly who he is, and why he is included here.

And finally, deep and abiding gratitude to the Spirits of Place, the Ancestors and the Land, the voices on the breeze, of bird, tree and bee and of the Awen that flows between.

'Be Thou Kind!'

Printed in Poland
by Amazon Fulfillment
Poland Sp. z o.o., Wrocław

53679674R00030